Published by Atmosphere
Willis Vean
Mullion Cornwall TR12 7DF
England
Tel 01326 240180

All images Copyright Bob Croxford 2008
Book Design and typography by Bob Croxford Copyright Atmosphere 2008
Printed and bound in Italy

ISBN 978-0-9550805-3-1

Many of the pictures in this and other Atmosphere books are available as large photo prints to frame. For details of sizes and prices see www.atmosphere.co.uk/prints.html

SIR FRANCIS DRAKE

PLYMOUTH

Plymouth is a city which has seen more than its share of history. It bears the scars of war and the memories of persecution and suffering. It also rejoices in some of the greatest events ever witnessed.

From very early times there were human settlements in nearby caves and at the mouth of the Plym river close by. When the River Plym became silted in Saxon times a new area was occupied on the site which is now the Barbican. Incursions by the French during the 100 Years War and later, led to the construction of fortifications.

In the 16th century Plymouth saw growth as a trading port. Two of the prominent men who had a profound effect on the City of Plymouth were Sir John Hawkins and Sir Francis Drake. Both of them were engaged in trade but more truthfully were privateers or legalised pirates authorised by Elizabeth I to attack and take Spanish ships for the treasure they were bringing back from the New World. Hawkins turned his hand to anything with a profit attached and was an early slave trader. His first slave trip resulted from attacking and taking a Portuguese slave ship and continuing the voyage to sell the slaves in Santo Domingo. He later became treasurer and controller of the Navy and introduced many improvements in ship construction.

Drake was the leader of the first British expedition around the world which set sail in 1577 with a crew of mostly Plymouth sailors. Despite many setbacks he managed to seize Spanish ships and battle his way around South America via the Magellan Strait. He was blown so far south by a storm that his small fleet became the first to enter the Antarctic. Reduced to one ship, The Golden Hind, he sailed north along the South American coast. Along the way he attacked Spanish towns and seized their treasure ships. After many more adventures he rounded the Cape of Good Hope in 1580 and arrived

The CUSTOM HOUSE coat of arms.

The entrance to SUTTON HARBO

back in Plymouth on September 26th. The whole town rushed to greet him and his remaining crew of 59. The Queen's share of the treasure was greater than her income from other sources for an entire year.

Knighted by the Queen, Sir Francis Drake had more fame to follow. As well as frequent raids on his shipping, Philipe II of Spain got tired of England's interference and encouragement of Protestantism in the Netherlands, which then belonged to Spain. He decided to invade England and return the country to the Roman Catholic faith. At the time Spain had the world's greatest navy and the Spanish Armada which set sail in 1588 was a formidable force. According to legend Drake continued a game of bowls on Plymouth Hoe while the Spanish massed in sight of the town. Drake's knowledge of tide and weather, when he did set sail, soon gave him an advantage over the Spanish whom he harried up the English Channel. With the aid of Hawkins the Armada was defeated.

Tourists flock to the spot at Sutton Harbour where in 1620 the Mayflower set sail for America carrying the Pilgrim separatists to their new home. Actually the Mayflower also set sail from Southampton and Dartmouth and stopped again in Newlyn for water before commencing the 66 day voyage but it is with Plymouth that the Mayflower is most associated. Although they are sometimes described as a brave band of settlers the Pilgrims were an ill equipped group of middle class dilettantes who travelled with 18 servants and another five hired helpers.

Others who left England from Plymouth were convicts bound for Australia. Two transport ships the 'Friendship' and the 'Charlotte' left in 1787 to establish the penal colony at Sydney. New Zealand was discovered and colonised by ships sailing from Plymouth.

Between 1755 and 1759 one of the most influential buildings of the Industrial age was constructed 14 miles out to sea on the Eddystone Rock. The lighthouse built by John Smeaton was a true 'tour de force'. Not only

Bowling Green sign on THE HOE.

was it built on rocks which barely rose above sea level but many revolutionary techniques were used in its construction. Despite the many technical difficulties that had to be overcome Smeaton remained a perfectionist. He fretted that the structure leant a little when a plumb

line suspended 50 feet to the floor was found to be one eighth of an inch out of true. It stood as a warning to shipping for over 100 years and was eventually replaced when the rock on which it was built showed signs of erosion. The top section was dismantled and re-erected on Plymouth Hoe as a fitting memorial to the father of civil engineering.

It can be said that the growth and shape of Plymouth was decided by the Navy Dockyard. The first Royal Dockyard opened in 1690 on the banks of the Tamar Estuary and was expanded several times over the next 100 years. Substantial storerooms and offices were built to administer the Docks some of which have now been converted into private dwellings. In the days of sailing ships Plymouth was at a distinct advantage over more easterly ports because less tacking was required against the prevailing south-westerly wind.

The Plymouth Blitz was a series of raids by Nazi German bombers targeting the Naval Docks. In just seven nights starting on March 20th 1941 the centres of Plymouth and Devonport were almost completely destroyed. As wave after wave of bombers swept over

Plymouth they met with little resistance except for a scattering of anti-aircraft guns placed to best protect the docks. Unfortunately these were situated to hit the planes before they reached their target. As the planes met the fire from these guns most of the terrified pilots dropped their bombs early. Instead of hitting the docks a huge number of bombs hit the city centre. Civilians suffered 1,172 deaths and 4,448 injured while the damage to the docks was never sufficient to stop their operation. Charles Church which was destroyed by incendiary bombs on the nights of March 20th and 21st 1941 remains in a ruined state as a memorial to the civilian dead.

The blitz shaped the look of modern Plymouth. With almost everything destroyed the post war planners decided to rebuild on a modern grid system. Areas of

narrow winding streets and lanes were swept away to allow the complete rebuilding of the central shopping district. Perhaps unfortunately the money available after the war was insufficient to rebuild everything to a high quality but with imaginative pedestrianisation and superior building when opportunity allows, Plymouth is morphing into an attractive modern city. The modern Theatre Royal was opened in 1982. It is a major showplace for drama, opera, ballet and musicals. A more recent development has been the Drake Circus Shopping Centre.

One of the few old buildings left in the centre is the Merchant's House dating from the 16th century which is now open as a museum.

When Plymouth was centred round the Sutton Harbour area it was occasionally raided by French incursions. For protection a small fort was built. Little now remains of this early structure but the name, The Barbican, which means a fortified gateway. The Barbican area is now a lively area of boats, shops, pubs and restaurants and with its cobbled streets is a reminder of what Plymouth was like many years ago. The harbour has been the centre of Plymouth's fishing fleet for centuries but fish quotas have cut seriously into the amount landed. The new Fish Market and the National Marine Aquarium are part of the regeneration of this part of the City. The Aquarium was built to provide education, conservation and research into our marine habitat and includes Britain's deepest fish tank holding 2.5 million litres of water.

Mount Batten is a defensive rocky hill to the east of the old Plymouth harbour. Recent excavations here have shown that this was the oldest trading site in Britain and the route for continental imports from the late Bronze Age and also in Roman times. It was a flying boat base for both the Royal Navy and the Royal Air Force and was joined by the Australian Air Force in WWII.

There is something very stylish about Plymouth's Art Deco Lido called the Tinside Pool. Built on rocks next to the sea below The Hoe in 1935 it became neglected and was closed in 1992. Revamped and renovated it was re-opened in 2005.

Brunel's Bridge above the River Tamar is one of the

great, iconic feats of Victorian engineering. 20,000 people turned up to see the first span launched and jacked into place. The site Foreman sent a boat up and down both banks with a man with a megaphone who shouted, "Mr Brunel will have a bit of hush." They all were silent as Isambard Kingdom Brunel supervised the raising of the span to bridge the river with his daring design. In doing so he created one of the greatest bridges in Britain. Named the Royal Albert Bridge by the prince who opened it in 1859 it was Brunel's last project before his death later that year,

Opposite Plymouth on the Cornish side of the estuary

lies the town of Saltash. The town developed as a port and important gateway to the upper reaches of the River Tamar. One of the most memorable sites to the passengers crossing the Tamar bridges is the highly decorated Union Inn which has a Union flag on the front face.

Much of the upper reaches of the rivers Tamar and Tavy are used to service Plymouth. The Lopwell Dam on the River Tavy was built in 1953 to provide an extra source of fresh water for the city. The dam and its surroundings are now a Local Nature Reserve.

The River Tamar curves in a series of gentle loops on its way to the sea. Compared to the bustle of Plymouth the area is quiet and peaceful.

Calstock on the River Tamar is dominated by a magnificent railway viaduct which spans the steep sided valley. The river is easily navigable here at high tide.

Cotehele House is one of The National Trust's finest properties. The estate reaches down to the edge of the river where the restored and preserved sailing barge 'Shamrock' is moored.

THE RIVER TAMAR at Calstock up-river from PLYMOUTH.

An aerial view of PLYMOUTH showing the TINSIDE POOL and SMEATON'S TOWER standing on THE HOE

e Annual Firework Competition lights up the sky behind SMEATON'S TOWER.

SMEATON'S TOWER 13

SMEATON'S TOWER dominates the view from THE HOE

A lasting monument to a great engineer, JOHN SMEATON.

Aerial view of THE HOE showing the TINSIDE POOL and SMEATON'S TOW

WEST HOE PIER is a popular spot for anglers.

A sailing boat glides past the restored ROYAL WILLIAM DOCKYARD

The grand entrance to ROYAL WILLIAM DOCKYARD

THE MERCHANT'S HOUSE is a fine 16th century Town House.

A cobbled corner .

The MAYFLOWER STEPS mark the spot near where the Pilgrim Fathers finally set sail in the Mayflower for the New Wor

SOUTHSIDE STREET in the BARBICAN area.   PLYMOUTH GIN from these premises is famous the world o'

PH 598

SUTTON HARBOUR is home to a variety of fishing and pleasure b

...g boats and converted warehouses reflected in SUTTON HARBOUR.

'THE PRAWN' a whimsical sculpture on SUTTON HARBOUR created by Partnership Art.   The NATIONAL MARINE AQUARI

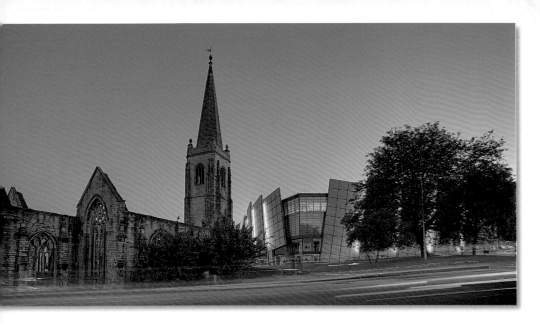

THEATRE ROYAL at night.   The ruined CHARLES CHURCH is a memorial to civilian casualties in WW2

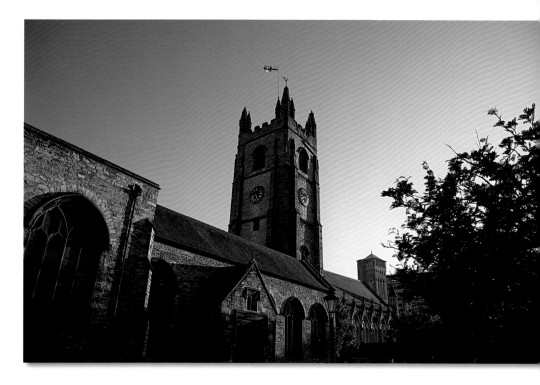

The restored church of ST ANDREW

The view from MOUNT BATTEN towards THE H

e breakwater at MOUNT BATTEN acts as a pier for anglers and strollers.

ticing water at the TINSIDE POOL.

The TINSIDE POOL with a Brittany Ferries ship leaving for Roscoff.

A trip on a cruise boat gives fine views of PLYMOUT

A sailing boat passes DRAKE'S ISLAND.

The TORPOINT FERRY is busy all day lc

e modern NAVAL DOCKYARD is a maintenance centre for the Royal Navy and also a harbour for Navy Ships.

The UNION INN at SALTASH.

Swans glide under the two bridges spanning the TAMAR RIV

MOUNT EDGECOMBE is situated on the Cornwall side of the TAMAR ESTUARY.   Two bridges span the TAMAR at SALTA

ALTON QUAY on the extreme left of this aerial view.　　　A curve in the RIVER TAMAR leads to GUNNISLAKE.

A stone causeway enables walkers to cross the RIVER TAVY below LOPWELL DA

OPWELL DAM on the RIVER TAVY.

CALSTOCK VIADUCT carries the railway line across the RIVER TAMA

A cottage in CALSTOCK

A rural road in the TAMAR VAL

The sailing barge SHAMROCK at COTEHELE QUAY.

NDEX

rleaf : Typical landscape above the TAMAR VALLEY.